BELLE PRATER'S BOY

by
Ruth White

Student Packet

Written by
Anne Troy

Contains masters for:

- 1   Prereading Activity
- 1   Study Guide
- 5   Vocabulary Activities
- 2   Literary Analysis Activities
- 6   Writing Activities
- 5   Quizzes/Tests
  (Vocabulary, 2 Objective, Multiple Choice, Short Answer/Essay)

Plus   Detailed Answer Key

Note

The Yearling Newbery paperback edition of the book, published by Bantam Doubleday Dell, was used to prepare this guide. The page references may differ in other editions.

Please note: Please assess the appropriateness of this book for the age level and maturity of your students prior to reading and discussing it with your class.

ISBN 1-58130-558-3

Copyright infringement is a violation of Federal Law.

© 2000, 2004 by Novel Units, Inc., Bulverde, Texas. All rights reserved. No part of this publication may be reproduced, translated, stored in a retrieval system, or transmitted in any way or by any means (electronic, mechanical, photocopying, recording, or otherwise) without prior written permission from Novel Units, Inc.

Photocopying of student worksheets by a classroom teacher at a non-profit school who has purchased this publication for his/her own class is permissible. Reproduction of any part of this publication for an entire school or for a school system, by for-profit institutions and tutoring centers, or for commercial sale is strictly prohibited.

Novel Units is a registered trademark of Novel Units, Inc.

Printed in the United States of America.

To order, contact your local school supply store, or—

Novel Units, Inc.
P.O. Box 97
Bulverde, TX 78163-0097

Web site: www.educyberstor.com

Name_____

Belle Prater's Boy
Activity #1: Anticipation Guide
Use Before Reading

Directions
Rate each of the following statements before you read the novel. In a small group, discuss your ratings and compare with those of others. After you have completed the novel, rate the statements again. Have any of your opinions changed?

```
1-----------------2-----------------3-----------------4-----------------5-----------------6
agree                                                                            disagree
strongly                                                                         strongly
```

                                                                                      Before   **After**

1. Every child needs two parents.   _____ _____

2. A stepfather can really understand a child.   _____ _____

3. Being angry is part of grieving.   _____ _____

4. Talking about it is a good way to handle the loss of a loved one.   _____ _____

5. Grandparents shouldn't be expected to look after their grandchildren.   _____ _____

6. There isn't much we can learn from old people—their ideas are too outdated.   _____ _____

7. The advantage of a small town is that everyone knows everyone else's life story.   _____ _____

8. A sense of humor helps in tough situations.   _____ _____

9. A homely person has to overcome a handicap.   _____ _____

10. You can't judge a book by its cover, or you can't judge a person only by appearances.   _____ _____

11. Use words, not fists.   _____ _____

12. Don't sit around feeling sorry for yourself.   _____ _____

13. Bullies are cowards at heart.   _____ _____

© Novel Units, Inc.   All rights reserved

Name_____

Belle Prater's Boy
Activity #2: Journal Writing
Use Before Reading

Directions
Complete each of the following sentence-starters, using the back of the paper if you need more space. Share your responses after reading the story and see how your ideals connect with the book.

1. People start calling each other names…

2. When a mother leaves a child…

3. When I kid around with my mom…

4. Kids who grow up being given everything they want…

5. Forgiveness…

6. When a bully bothers you…

7. What you can tell by how a person looks and dresses is…

8. Living in a rural small town…

9. Standing up for what you feel is right…

10. Grandkids can learn much from grandparents when…

11. When something tragic happens to someone from school, most kids…

12. If I ever lost my parents…

© Novel Units, Inc.   All rights reserved

Name_____

Belle Prater's Boy
Study Questions
Use During Reading

Directions
Write a brief answer to each study question as you read the book at home or in class. Use the questions for review before group discussion and before your final exam.
* Marks an open-ended question; no right or wrong answers

Chapters 1–2 (Pages 3–22)
1. What is the setting (time and place) in which the story opens? What is the setting on page 16?
2. Who is the narrator of the story?
3. What is the problem at the beginning of the novel?
4. Why is Woodrow living with his grandparents?
5. What do we know about Gypsy? How is she related to Woodrow?
6. What is Gypsy's problem with her stepfather, Porter?
7. *Prediction:* How will Gypsy resolve her problem with Porter?*

Chapters 3–4 (Pages 23–38)
1. How do Woodrow's grandparents treat him? How do you think they treated their daughters, Love and Belle?*
2. What do the men in the barbershop say that might hurt Woodrow? Gypsy?
3. How important is Gypsy's hair to her mother? To her?
4. In what way is Gypsy like her Aunt Belle?
5. What makes the birthday party special for Woodrow?
6. Why do you think that Belle left a beautiful house and happy family to live in a shack?*
7. *Prediction:* What does Woodrow want most? How will the problem of his mother's disappearance be solved?*

Chapters 5–6 (Pages 39–57)
1. Who took Aunt Belle's boyfriend? What effect did this have on Aunt Belle?
2. Why did Belle marry Everett Prater?
3. Why did Belle think she had to get away?*

© Novel Units, Inc.   All rights reserved

Name_____   **Belle Prater's Boy**
Study Questions
page 2

4. Give some examples of Gypsy's childlike behavior. When does she act like a grown-up?
5. Who insults Woodrow by talking about his mama and his looks? Why do you think she does this?*
6. What secrets do Woodrow and Gypsy share in the tree house?
7. Why do Woodrow and Gypsy decide to meet at the tree house after everyone else is in bed?
8. *Prediction:* What will Woodrow explain about his mother's disappearance?*

Chapters 7–8 (Pages 58–74)

1. Explain the strange place that Woodrow calls the place "where two worlds touch."* (page 60)
2. Who is Blind Benny? How important do you think he will be in the story?*
3. Who was Ed Morrell? How did Belle compare herself to Ed Morrell?
4. If Belle left on her own, why did she leave Woodrow behind?*
5. Who finds Gypsy on her way back from the tree house in the middle of the night?
6. How is Woodrow helping Gypsy?
7. How does Woodrow handle the first day at school? How does he show that he is not shy and really quite clever?
8. *Prediction:* How will Woodrow's preoccupation with his mother's disappearance affect his life?*

Chapters 9–10 (Pages 75–90)

1. Why does Everett Prater come to visit? How does Woodrow treat his dad?
2. What disturbs Woodrow when he looks out the window while his father gets into the car?
3. Why does Gypsy accept Porter's invitation to go to the movies? What upsets her at the movie?
4. How is Gypsy's episode at the movie related to her nightmare?

© Novel Units, Inc.   All rights reserved

Name_____

Belle Prater's Boy
Study Questions
page 3

5. *Prediction:* What is the ugly thing in Gypsy's dream? What do you think Doc means when he says "…her father"? What do Gypsy's dreams have to do with her father?* (page 88)

Chapters 11–12 (Pages 91–109)
1. Why do you think Woodrow brings Blind Benny to visit Gypsy while she is sick?*
2. What does Gypsy learn from Benny that she does not want to remember?
3. What does Benny's remark, "Too bad what happened to him!" mean? (page 95)
4. Why do you think Gypsy resents Porter so much?*
5. How does Woodrow believe his mother will contact him?
6. What happens at the campfire party? How does Buzz try to spoil the party?
7. *Prediction:* What kinds of trouble could Woodrow get into?*

Chapters 13–14 (Pages 110–123)
1. How does Woodrow make up for his lack of good looks?
2. What does Gypsy learn about her hair and her father that she did not know?
3. What mistakes do you think Grandpa and Granny made in raising Belle and Love?*
4. How does Woodrow react to Gypsy's question about Uncle Everett having something to do with the disappearance of Aunt Belle?
5. What are some of the examples of "where the two worlds touch"? (pages 122–123)
6. Why do you think Woodrow checks the personal ads?*
7. *Prediction:* Where do you think Belle Prater is?*

Chapters 15–16 (Pages 124–144)
1. How does Woodrow change the summer for Gypsy?
2. How is Woodrow's life different in town than it had been in the holler?*

Name_____

Belle Prater's Boy
Study Questions
page 4

3. Why does Mrs. Cooper pick on Woodrow at the party?

4. Do you think Woodrow is trying to get even with Mrs. Cooper when he tries the "power of suggestion" on her?* (page 132)

5. Why does the "power of suggestion" work on Mrs. Cooper, but not on Woodrow's father?

6. What stirs up Gypsy's jealousy?

7. What do you think Woodrow means when he says, "It wasn't him that left you!"?* (page 139)

8. What is the moral of the story about the girl with long, golden hair? Why does the story make Gypsy angry?

9. How does Porter compare Belle and Gypsy?

10. What does Porter think happened to Belle?

11. *Prediction:* How or when will Gypsy see that Porter is a good man?*

Chapters 17–18 (Pages 145–162)

1. How have Gypsy's nightmares changed?

2. What does Buzz suggest that Woodrow tell the class and the teacher?

3. Do you think the invisible brew story explains what happened to Belle?*

4. What untrue things does Gypsy tell about her father's death?

5. What reasons does Buzz give for Amos Leemaster's suicide?

6. How does Gypsy react to the scene at school?

7. Why does Gypsy cut her hair?

8. How does Porter find Gypsy? How does he treat her?

9. *Prediction:* What will Gypsy's mother say about her short hair?*

Chapters 19–20 (Pages 163–174)

1. Why hadn't Gypsy and her mother talked about Amos Leemaster's suicide?

2. Why did Amos Leemaster commit suicide?

3. How does Gypsy try to explain her short hair?

4. Is Gypsy a coward for not going to school the day after Buzz and Woodrow's fight?*

© Novel Units, Inc.   All rights reserved

Name_____

Belle Prater's Boy
Study Questions
page 5

5. What is the "parasite, feeding on [Gypsy's] grief"?* (page 166)
6. How does Gypsy "paint herself into a corner"? (page 168)
7. How does Gypsy turn her embarrassment over her extremely short hair into something for every girl to imitate?
8. How do you think Gypsy has changed?*
9. What kind of person do you think Gypsy will be when she grows up?*

Chapters 21–23 (Pages 175–196)
1. How did Blind Benny get food after his parents died? What is a superstition?
2. How had Love and Amos Leemaster helped Blind Benny? Why does Blind Benny make his nightly rounds?
3. What Sunday school story does Gypsy recall? Who does Gypsy think might be Jesus in disguise?
4. What experiences do Woodrow and Gypsy want to relive?
5. What is the impulsive thing that Gypsy does for Benny?
6. What does Woodrow mean when he says, "...Blind Benny, even with his poor sightless eyes, is the only person I know who can see with perfect clarity"? (page 186)
7. What are the important announcements at Granny Ball's birthday dinner?
8. What does Woodrow mean when he says, "...I have learned a beautiful place can't shelter you from hurt any more than a shack can"? (page 192)
9. What stories does Woodrow say his mother made up? Does Woodrow know the difference between reality and make-believe? Prove it.
10. What facts about Belle's disappearance does Woodrow reveal? Why hasn't Woodrow told his father about the missing clothes and money?
11. How does Woodrow compare his father to the farmer in the golden-hair story?
12. Why does Woodrow always read the personal ads in the Sunday paper?
13. How does Gypsy compare Belle and her father?
14. What are the in-between feelings that Gypsy and Woodrow have?

© Novel Units, Inc.   All rights reserved

Name_____

Belle Prater's Boy
Activity #3: Vocabulary
Chapters 1–4

"Guess Word"

Object of the Game: Guess the word on the card your partner is holding.
Step 1: Students form pairs.
Step 2: Cut out two identical sets of vocabulary cards (below), one set for each player.

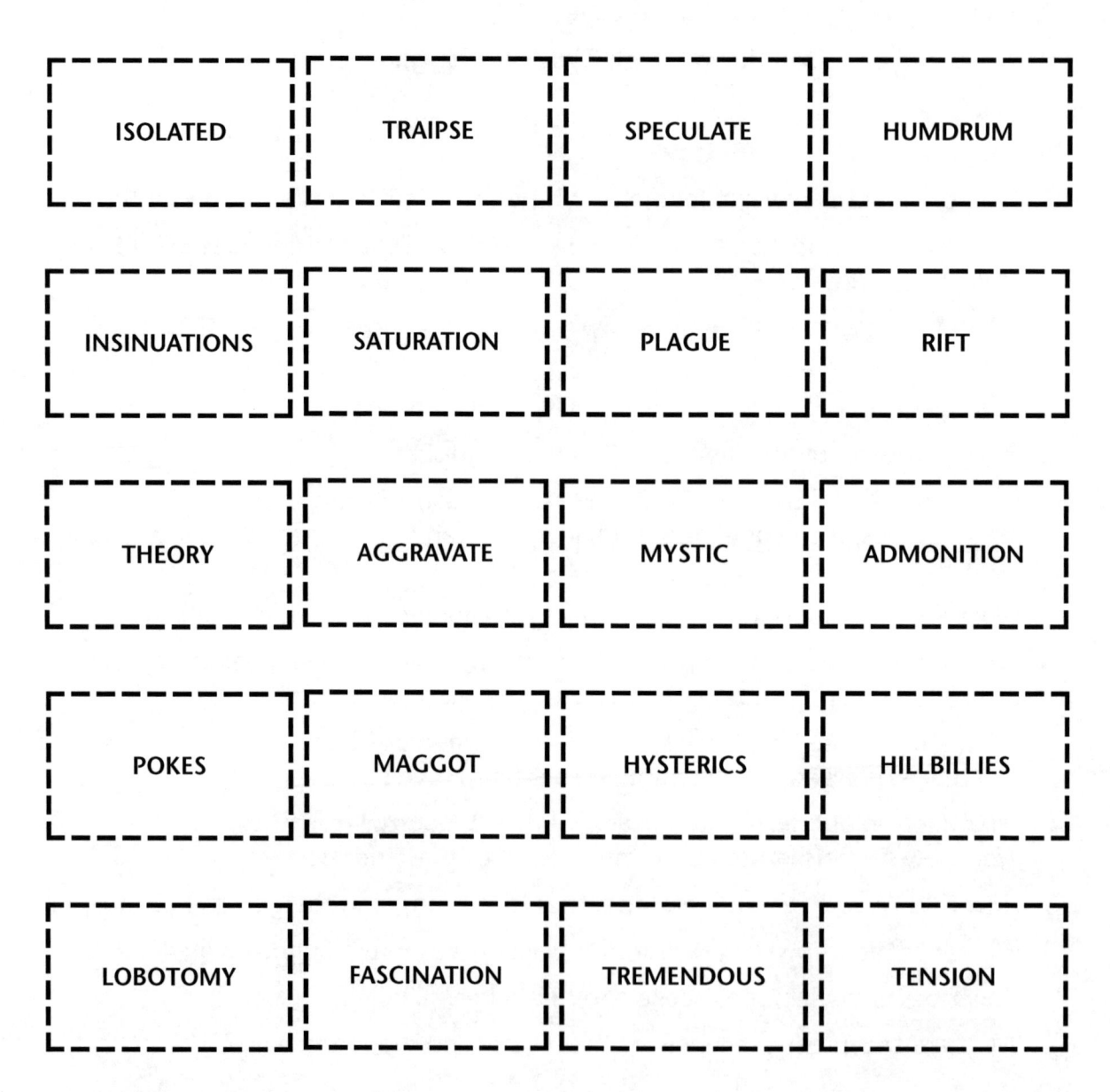

ISOLATED	TRAIPSE	SPECULATE	HUMDRUM
INSINUATIONS	SATURATION	PLAGUE	RIFT
THEORY	AGGRAVATE	MYSTIC	ADMONITION
POKES	MAGGOT	HYSTERICS	HILLBILLIES
LOBOTOMY	FASCINATION	TREMENDOUS	TENSION

Step 3: Each player lays out his or her cards face down.

© Novel Units, Inc.   All rights reserved

Name_____

Belle Prater's Boy
Activity #3: Vocabulary
page 2

Step 4: Each player picks up one word card and puts it aside. (This is the word the partner tries to guess.)

Step 5: Players flip a coin to see who goes first.

Step 6: The player who is up gets to ask one yes-or-no question about the word the other player has chosen. (e.g., Is the word a noun? Does the word mean "lively"? Does the word have more than two syllables?)

Step 7: Based on the answer to the question, the player turns over all of his or her cards that cannot be in in the other player's hand.
Players may refer to the novel and to a dictionary before answering yes-or-no questions. Play continues until one player guesses the other player's word. (If the player guesses incorrectly at any point, he or she forfeits a turn.)

Blank cards:

Name_____

Belle Prater's Boy
Activity #4: Vocabulary
Chapters 5–10

mesmerized 40	conjured 53	straitjacket 63	follicles 86
immature 43	swashbuckling 53	mattock 78	sedative 87
reckless 43	invisible 55	dissected 81	frenzy 88
ample 52	resolution 56	compulsion 81	inevitable 88
stash 53	addled 61	option 85	

Examine the words in the box above and use a dictionary to look up any you cannot define. Then use the chart below to classify each word according to how you think the author might use it in the novel: to describe the Setting (time and place), Characters (what they are like), Characters' Actions (what they do), and Problems. Also classify the words as nouns, verbs, adjectives, and adverbs.

CHARACTERS

CHARACTERS' ACTIONS

SETTING

PROBLEMS

OTHER

© Novel Units, Inc.

All rights reserved

Name_____

Belle Prater's Boy
Activity #5: Vocabulary
Chapters 11–16

Directions
Underline or circle the word or phrase that *least* belongs with the others and briefly explain why it does not belong.

1. flabbergasted — astounded — dedicated — amazed
2. microscopic — burly — minute — small
3. hardheaded — shrewd — obstinate — disfigured
4. abdomen — appendage — paunch — stomach
5. exasperated — annoyed — irritated — appeased
6. agitate — tranquilize — disturb — disorder
7. impulsive — spontaneous — premeditated — impetuous
8. stalk — track — stampede — pursue
9. commence — begin — start — remember
10. exotic — natural — foreign — strange
11. inevitable — unavoidable — certain — avoidable
12. delectable — choice — distasteful — tasty
13. retaliate — retort — reward — revenge
14. rabid — sweet — crazed — deranged
15. astound — marvel — overwhelm — repulsive

© Novel Units, Inc. All rights reserved

Name_____

Belle Prater's Boy
Activity #6: Vocabulary
Chapters 17–23

Directions

Put the words below into alphabetical order. Then use a dictionary to find a brief definition, a phonetic spelling, and a word origin. Write these in the proper columns. On the back of your paper, number from 1 to 10. Explain in your own words the significance of each vocabulary word to *Belle Prater's Boy*.

trekked 146	nonchalantly 153	agitated 153	exertion 159
remorse 160	disfigurement 164	parasite 166	bombarded 173
elated 174	consumption 177		

Word	Definition	Phonetic Spelling	Origin

© Novel Units, Inc.   All rights reserved

Name_____ *Belle Prater's Boy*
Activity #7: Vocabulary

The Great Prefix and Suffix Search

1. Use these suffixes to make nouns: -ion, -ment, -ise, -ance. Find examples from the book and examples from your own experiences.

   _____   _____   _____

   _____   _____   _____

   _____   _____   _____

2. These suffixes are used to make adjectives: -ful and -ous. Locate several examples.

   _____   _____   _____

   _____   _____   _____

   _____   _____   _____

3. What do these prefixes mean? Find examples of each.

   Prefix Meaning   **Examples**

   in-   _____   _____

   inter-   _____   _____

   ex-   _____   _____

   trans-   _____   _____

   non-   _____   _____

   dis-   _____   _____

© Novel Units, Inc.   All rights reserved

Name_____   ***Belle Prater's Boy***
                                                 Activity #8: Writing to Explain and Describe

Directions
Write the first draft of an essay using attribute webs you have developed for Woodrow and Gypsy. Your essay should look something like this:

Paragraph 1: Provide background on the story (title, author, one-line summary), and introduce your thesis (a general statement about the relationship of the two characters)

Paragraph 2: Explain how Woodrow and Gypsy feel about each other when Woodrow first comes to live with his grandparents.

Paragraph 3: Explain how their relationship evolves.

Paragraph 4: Explain how their jealousy comes to a head.

Paragraph 5: Conclusion—Summarize and emphasize your thesis. (How do Gypsy and Woodrow resolve their problems?)

Title: Give your essay a title that states or refers to your thesis.

Evaluation: Use the rubric below to evaluate your essay.

---

1. Does the first word in every sentence begin with a capital?
2. Does every sentence end with a period, question mark, or exclamation point?
3. Did I correct each run-on by making it into at least two sentences?
4. Did I correct each fragment by making it into a sentence that can stand alone?
5. Did I indent the first word of each paragraph?
6. Do all sentences in the paragraph tell about the same thing?
7. Did I check for words that look as if they are spelled wrong?
8. Did I read the whole piece of writing aloud to check for errors?

© Novel Units, Inc.   All rights reserved

Name_____

Belle Prater's Boy
Activity #9: Writing and Characterization

Characterization

Characterization is the way a writer lets the reader know what the characters are like. In direct characterization, the writer describes the person and his or her physical characteristics. In indirect characterization, the writer provides clues about the character through thoughts, speech, and actions.

Directions
Choose one of the characters. Use direct and indirect characterization as techniques you use to describe that character in writing. On the back of this sheet of paper, draw the character you describe.

Name_____   ***Belle Prater's Boy***
                                         Activity #10: Writing Personal Narration

Gypsy and her mother have a heart-to-heart talk about Amos Leemaster's suicide and Gypsy's reaction. Love explains, *"We didn't talk about it because we couldn't bear to....You just couldn't stand to look truth in the face..."* (page 164)

Assignment
Write a personal narrative about a time when you could not "look truth in the face."

1. Begin with a sentence announcing the purpose of your narrative. You are going to explain how, in your own personal experience, you could not face the truth. For example, you might begin your narrative with the statement, "I've always tried to tell the truth, but sometimes I can't face what the truth really is." Write your first sentence below.

   _____
   _____

2. A personal narrative tells about an experience you have had, usually describing events in the order in which they occurred. List the main events you want to tell about below. (Be sure they're listed in the order in which they happened.)

   _____
   _____
   _____
   _____

3. Before you begin writing, here are some other points to consider.
   *What things in your narrative will you need to describe (for example, the setting, something you really wanted, a person who interfered with reaching your goal or getting your wish)?
   *How do you feel about this experience now? What did you learn? Is there something you wish you would have done?

4. Write your narrative, beginning with the sentence in #1, then describing what happened, and ending with a concluding sentence.

5. When you finish writing, evaluate your narrative using the rubric below. Make any corrections you wish. Then have a partner or your peer editing group read your narrative and offer suggestions. Make any further changes and write your final draft.

© Novel Units, Inc.   All rights reserved

Name_____ *Belle Prater's Boy*
Activity #10: Writing Personal Narration
page 2

	OK	Change
Content		
1. Focus: Do all sentences in a paragraph tell about the same thing? Do all paragraphs develop the central idea?	_____	_____
2. Specificity: Have I used enough description to help my readers "see" what happened? Is my choice of words precise? Have I avoided repetition? Have I eliminated overused words and phrases?	_____	_____
3. Clarity: Is my purpose in writing clear? Has that purpose been accomplished?	_____	_____
4. Sequence: Is there a clear beginning, middle, and end? Are transitions used to connect one idea to the next?	_____	_____
Mechanics		
5. Are all words spelled correctly?	_____	_____
6. Have I used proper capitalization?	_____	_____
7. Are sentences punctuated correctly?	_____	_____
8. Do subjects and verbs agree?	_____	_____
9. Have I indented each paragraph?	_____	_____

Peer Editor
(Write your comments on the back of this sheet.)

1. Write one sentence summarizing what you think the writer is trying to say in this essay.

2. What is one thing you like about this piece?

3. Are sentences punctuated correctly?

4. What is one question you have about this piece?

© Novel Units, Inc.   All rights reserved

Name_____

Belle Prater's Boy
Activity #11: Poetry Writing
Use After Reading

Pyramid Poetry

Directions

Write a "pyramid poem" by filling in the blank lines in the diagram according to the chart. Share your poem with the rest of the group.

Line 1:	Name one of the main characters	Line 6:	Six words describing a second main event
Line 2:	Two words describing the character	Line 7:	Seven words describing a third main event
Line 3:	Three words describing the setting		
Line 4:	Four words stating the character's problem	Line 8:	Eight words stating how the character's problem is solved
Line 5:	Five words describing one main event		

© Novel Units, Inc.   All rights reserved

Name_____

Belle Prater's Boy
Activity #12: Critical Thinking/Decision Making
Use After Reading

Directions
Before Belle Prater decided to disappear, she must have thoughtfully weighed the reasons for and against such an action. List the reasons *for* and the reasons *against* doing this. (Include reasons mentioned in the novel, as well as others you can think

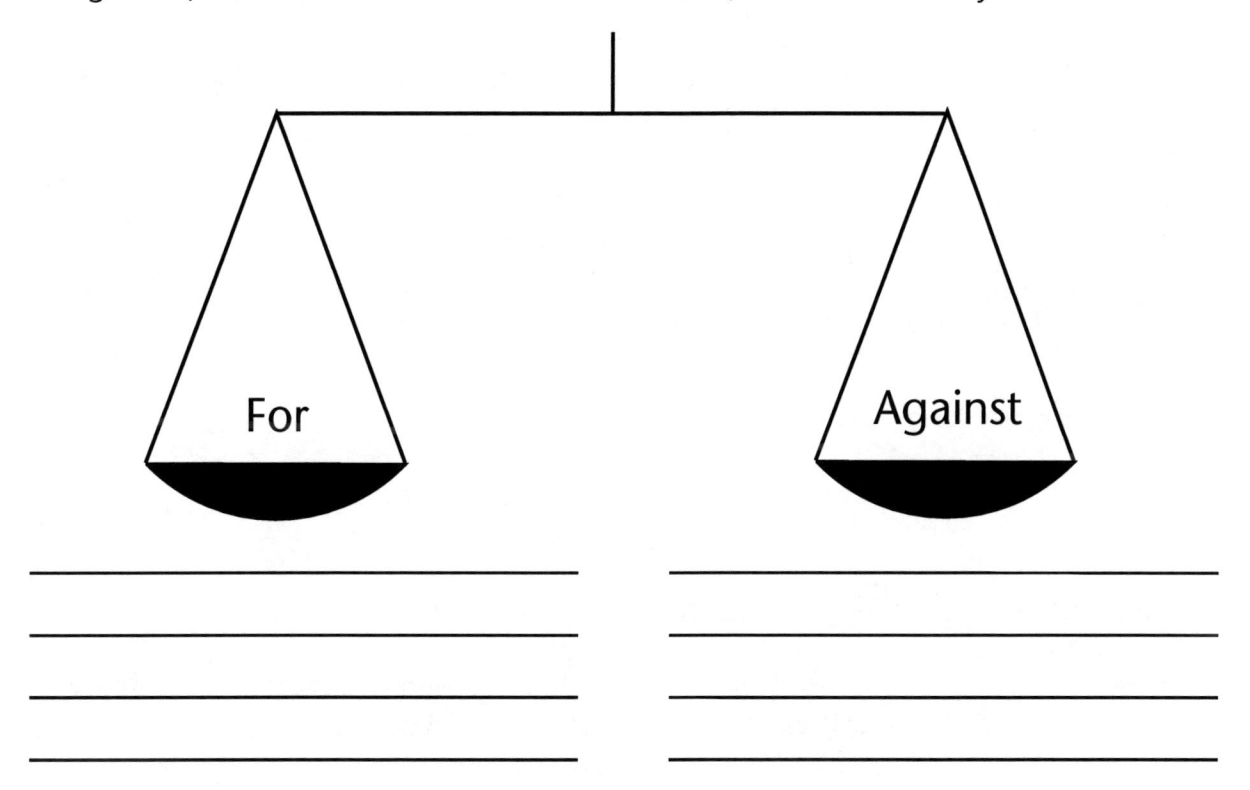

For | Against

_____ _____
_____ _____
_____ _____
_____ _____

What reason do you think is most compelling?

What other alternatives did Belle have?

Did Belle make the best choice? Explain why or why not in a short paragraph.

© Novel Units, Inc. All rights reserved

Name_____   *Belle Prater's Boy*
                                          Activity #13: Writing

Write an essay on how Gypsy changes and grows over the course of the novel. Several factors contribute to the changes and growth we see. Complete the graphic below by jotting down three causes for Gypsy's behavior and then completing the sentence about the overall change in Gypsy.

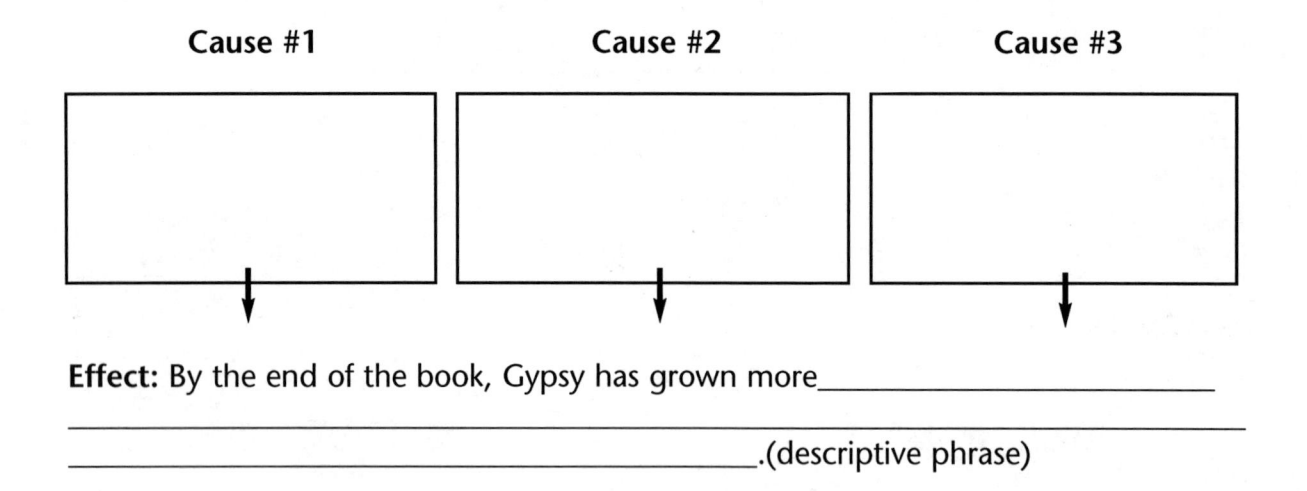

Cause #1	Cause #2	Cause #3

Effect: By the end of the book, Gypsy has grown more_____
_____
_____.(descriptive phrase)

As you write your first draft, consider organizing your ideas as follows:

    Paragraph 1: Introduction—Include the title, author, and who Gypsy Leemaster is. State your thesis (a brief generalization about how Gypsy changes).
    Paragraph 2: Incident #1 or Character Change #1
    Paragraph 3: Incident #2 or Character Change #2
    Paragraph 4: Incident #3 or Character Change #3
    Paragraph 5: Conclusion—Summarize the main points of your thesis. Leave your reader with something to "chew on." How is Gypsy going to be when she grows up? How will these incidents affect her entire life? How have these incidents improved the character of Gypsy? Is she a better or worse person because of these happenings in her life?

When you are finished, read your essay aloud to a partner or to a peer editing group.

Name_____

Belle Prater's Boy
Activity #14: Sociogram
Use During or After Reading

Directions

On the arrows pointing from Woodrow to the other characters, write how Woodrow feels/acts toward those characters. On the arrows leading from the characters back to Woodrow, write how those characters feel/act toward Woodrow.

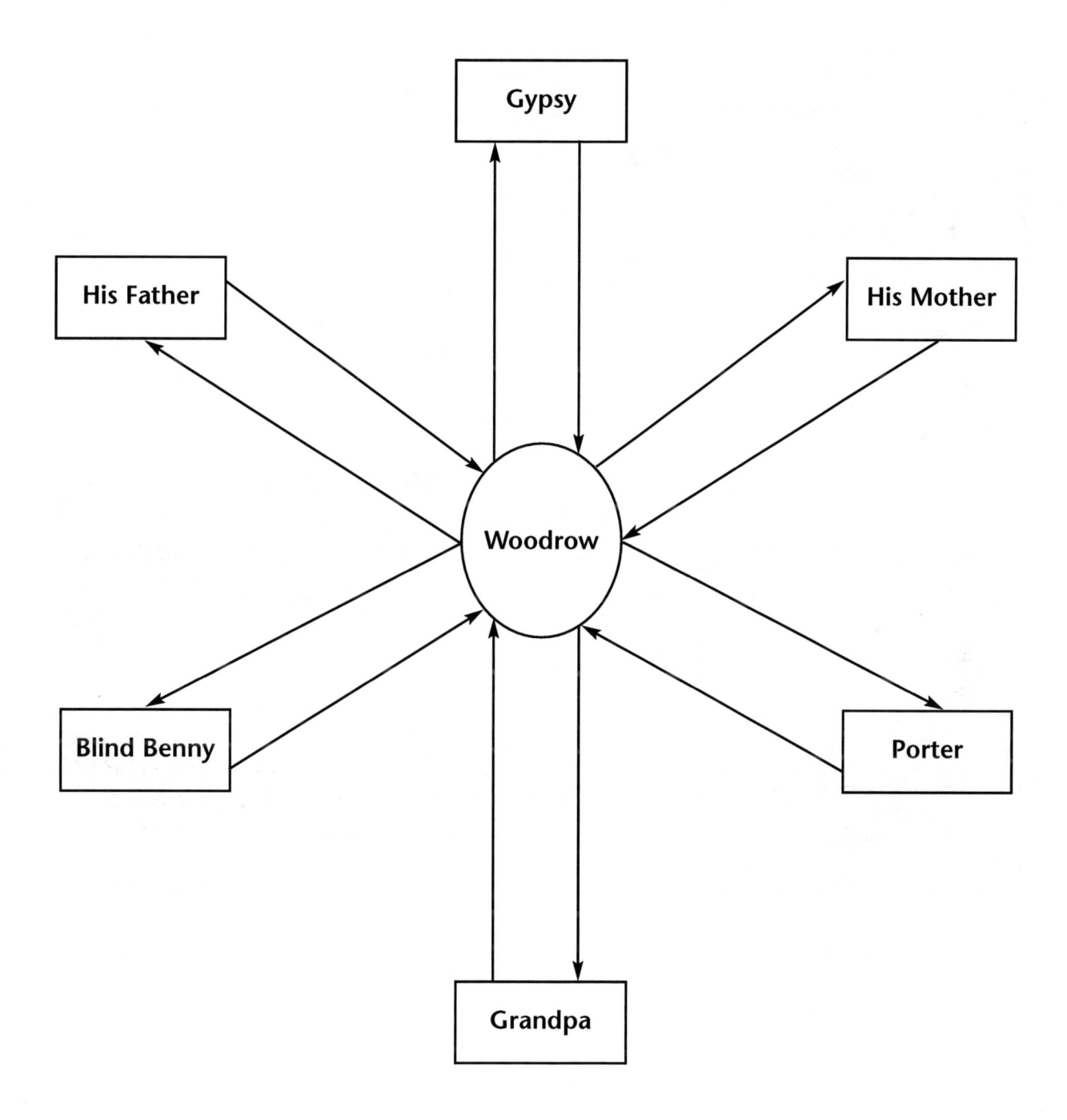

- Gypsy
- His Father
- His Mother
- Woodrow
- Blind Benny
- Porter
- Grandpa

Name_____

Belle Prater's Boy
Novel Test
Vocabulary

Directions
Match the correct definition to each word.

____1. lucid

____2. disfigurement

____3. nonchalantly

____4. agitated

____5. retaliation

____6. compulsion

____7. manipulate

____8. inevitable

____9. mesmerized

___10. conjured

___11. impulsive

___12. traipsing

___13. insinuations

___14. admonitions

___15. addled

A. call upon

B. revenge

C. confused

D. wandering, walking

E. bright, clear

F. certain, unavoidable

G. headlong, hasty, impetuous

H. lightheartedly

I. rebukes, warnings

J. ruffled, shaken

K. suggestions, hints

L. motivation

M. control, maneuver

N. profound

O. deformity, blemish

P. perpetual

Q. hypnotize

Name_____

Belle Prater's Boy
Novel Test
Objective

Identification

Find the character on the right who matches the description on the left. Write in the letter of the character in the blank provided.

____ 1. Cross-eyed boy who can tell great stories

____ 2. A woman whose pain is bigger than her love

____ 3. He wants to try an experiment of suggestion.

____ 4. She is saved from being buried alive by grave robbers.

____ 5. A singer who scavenges in the night

____ 6. A volunteer fireman who is burned trying to save a baby

____ 7. Tries to be the first one to read the paper on Sunday morning

____ 8. He wants to be a good stepfather.

____ 9. She wins over her sister's boyfriend and marries him.

____ 10. Her hair is a source of pride for her mother.

____ 11. Hard-headed boy who tries to spoil the campfire party

____ 12. A schoolteacher who sometimes lets his grammar slip back to mountain talk

____ 13. She tries to forget she found her father's body.

____ 14. She takes a boy's clothes and $30 to run away.

____ 15. Asks Love to promise not to cut Beauty's hair

A. Mrs. Cooper
B. Grandpa Ball
C. Gypsy
D. Belle Prater
E. Amos Leemaster
F. Granny Ball
G. Woodrow
H. Aunt Millie
I. Blind Benny
J. Porter
K. Love
L. Buzz
M. Mr. Collins
N. Everett Prater
O. Floyd Collins

© Novel Units, Inc.   All rights reserved

Name_____

Belle Prater's Boy
Novel Test
Identification

Identification by Quotation

Directions
Name the character who says each of the following quotations. Characters may be used more than once.

_____ 1. "The secret is hiding in the lines of this poem."

_____ 2. "And I have promised my sister in my heart that if I ever see her again, I will tell her how truly sorry I am that I caused her pain."

_____ 3. "They talk about my hair, but do they ever see what's underneath?"

_____ 4. "Don't look in there! Don't look in the window!"

_____ 5. "It's not so bad being blind…I don't have to look at ugly things."

_____ 6. "It's being filtered through two worlds. Some kind of real strong force field separating the two dimensions."

_____ 7. "Maybe them cockeyed stories the girls seem to like so much crossed your goofy eyes, huh?"

_____ 8. "It wuz *his* name for you! He always called you Beauty—short for Arbutus."

_____ 9. "I gotta feeling that would be a thing up with which your mama would not put."

_____ 10. "Pretty is as pretty does. That's saying that anybody who *does* pretty *is* pretty, and that ain't the truth."

_____ 11. "Nobody can outshine you if you can just be yourself. Belle never learned that, and it caused her a lot of grief."

_____ 12. "Order it, Mama…I want to learn how to be invisible."

_____ 13. "My mother said that Amos Leemaster got his face so scarred up in that fire you couldn't recognize him, and…"

© Novel Units, Inc.   All rights reserved

Name_____

Belle Prater's Boy
Novel Test
Multiple Choice

Directions
Circle the letter of the best response to the question.

1. What state is the setting for *Belle Prater's Boy*?
   A. New York
   B. California
   C. Virginia
   D. Alabama

2. The author of *Belle Prater's Boy* is
   A. Paula Danziger.
   B. E. L. Konigsburg.
   C. Ron Koertge.
   D. Ruth White.

3. The narrator of the story is
   A. Belle Prater.
   B. Woodrow.
   C. Amos Leemaster.
   D. Gypsy.

4. The problem at the beginning of the novel is
   A. Belle Prater has disappeared.
   B. Amos Leemaster has died.
   C. Grandpa Bell is deaf.
   D. Gypsy is jealous of her cousin Woodrow.

5. The thing most people would notice first about Gypsy would be
   A. her sense of humor.
   B. her beautiful hair.
   C. her talent for playing the piano.
   D. her relationship with her stepfather.

6. Belle and Love had problems in high school because
   A. Belle was an outstanding beauty.
   B. Love had more boyfriends and got more attention.
   C. Grandpa and Granny favored Love.
   D. Love made fun of Belle.

7. Belle ran off with Everett Prater because
   A. she loved him.
   B. her parents mistreated her.
   C. she thought she'd love living in Crooked Ridge.
   D. she couldn't face the fact that Love had taken her boyfriend, Amos.

© Novel Units, Inc.   All rights reserved

Name_____

Belle Prater's Boy
Multiple Choice
page 2

8. Which is not an effect of Belle Prater's marriage to Everett?
   A. She lived in poverty in Crooked Ridge.
   B. She did not have easy access to a piano and music.
   C. She had freedom.
   D. She pulled away from contact with her parents.

9. Gypsy has terrible dreams about
   A. finding her father after his suicide.
   B. animals chasing her.
   C. terrible storms.
   D. her father and mother quarreling.

10. Woodrow and Gypsy share secrets in the tree house. What does Woodrow want?
    A. To get A's in school
    B. To beat the other boys in wrestling
    C. His mother and straight eyes
    D. To get some new clothes so he won't look like a hillbilly

11. Gypsy does not like Porter because
    A. he is a cruel stepfather.
    B. he cannot take her father's place.
    C. he takes Love's attention away from Gypsy.
    D. he makes fun of her hair.

12. Porter gives Gypsy _____ when she is sick.
    A. a book
    B. a puzzle
    C. a radio and fan
    D. a dog

13. Amos Leemaster committed suicide because
    A. Love wanted to marry someone else.
    B. he was depressed and could not accept his disfigured appearance.
    C. he was in financial trouble.
    D. he had not saved the baby in the fire.

14. The type of conflict between Buzz and Woodrow is
    A. person against society.
    B. inner conflict.
    C. person against person.
    D. person against nature.

© Novel Units, Inc. All rights reserved

Name_____ *Belle Prater's Boy*
Multiple Choice
page 3

15. Belle Prater left Crooked Ridge because
    A. she did not love Woodrow.
    B. she felt trapped, like she was in a straitjacket.
    C. she wanted to meet Ed Morrell.
    D. she drank too much of the invisible recipe.

16. Belle uses the money she saved for Woodrow's eye surgery to
    A. buy new clothes.
    B. get a present for Woodrow.
    C. repair the old Ford.
    D. run away.

17. _____ says, "I have learned a beautiful place can't shelter you from hurt any more than a shack can."
    A. Gypsy
    B. Grandpa
    C. Woodrow
    D. Belle

18. _____ says, "…their pain was bigger than their love."
    A. Gypsy
    B. Granny
    C. Woodrow
    D. Porter

19. Blind Benny "can see with perfect clarity" because
    A. he is not really blind.
    B. he is able to see beyond appearances.
    C. he has special glasses.
    D. his seeing-eye dog helps him.

20. Woodrow chooses to try his experiment on Mrs. Cooper because
    A. she had been a close friend of his mother, Belle Prater.
    B. she does not drink much liquor, and is thus the perfect person.
    C. she is the life of the garden party.
    D. she is wearing a swimsuit.

Name_____

Belle Prater's Boy
Novel Test
Short Answer/Essay

Identification
Write a few sentences describing each character, thing, or place.

1. Crooked Ridge

2. tree house

3. Granny Ball

4. Love

5. Porter

6. Mr. Collins

7. Mrs. Cooper

8. Gypsy

9. Woodrow

10. Belle Prater

Essay
Choose two topics from A,B,C,D, and E. Write a well-organized essay of at least three paragraphs for each topic you choose. Be sure to include references and details from the novel.

    A. Describe the main conflicts in *Belle Prater's Boy*. Explain if and how each conflict is resolved.

© Novel Units, Inc.   All rights reserved

Name_____ **Belle Prater's Boy**
Short Answer/Essay
page 2

B. Family members have certain duties and responsibilities toward one another. Choose one of the family groups and explain whether or not members of this group meet their responsibilities.
   - Porter and Gypsy
   - Grandpa and Granny Ball
   - Love and Belle
   - Woodrow and Gypsy
   - Belle and Everett Prater

C. Explain what you think the author is saying about appearances.

D. Describe how each of the family members changes in the course of the story.

E. Compare and contrast two of the characters in the novel. For example: Belle/Love, Gypsy/Woodrow, or Gypsy/Belle. What conflicts do they both face? How are they different? Use the Venn diagram below to prepare the major points

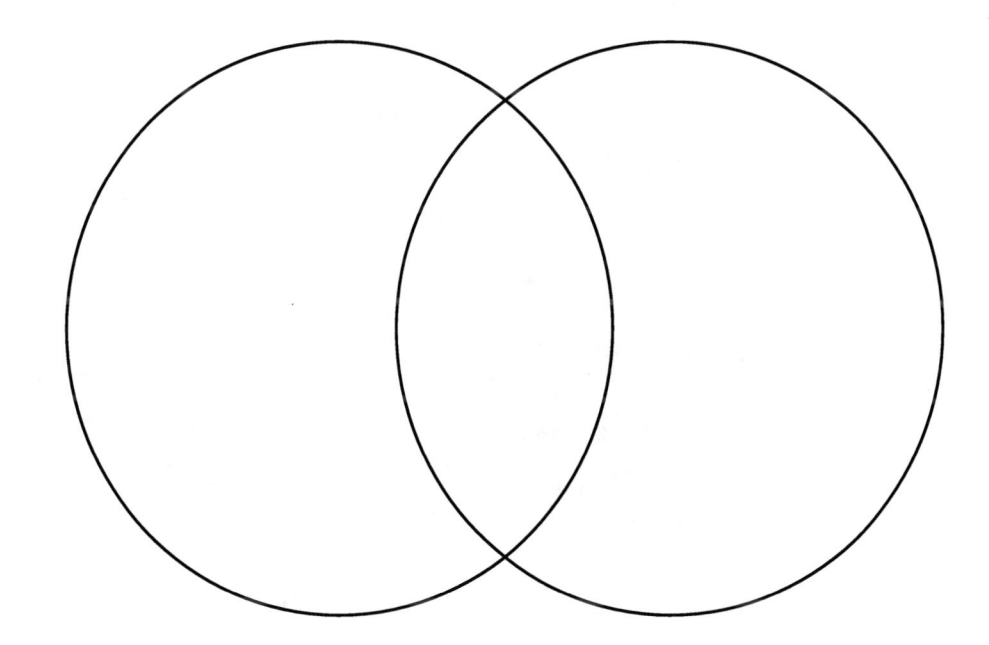

Name_____   *Belle Prater's Boy*
                                               Essay Evaluation

Essay Evaluation Form

1. **Focus:** Student writes a clear thesis and includes it in the opening paragraph.	10	8	4
2. **Organization:** The final draft reflects the assigned outline; transitions are used to link ideas.	20	16	12
3. **Support:** Adequate quotes are provided and are properly documented.	12	10	7
4. **Detail:** Each quote is explained (as if the teacher had not read the book); ideas are not redundant.	12	10	7
5. **Mechanics:** Spelling, capitalization, and usage are correct.	16	12	8
6. **Sentence Structure:** The student avoids run-ons and sentence fragments.	10	8	4
7. **Verbs:** All verbs are in the correct tense; sections in which plot is summarized are in the present tense.	10	8	4
8. **Total** effect of the essay.	10	8	4
	100	80	50

Comments:

Total:_____

(This rubric may be altered to fit the needs of a particular class. You may wish to show it to students before they write their essays. They can use it as a self-evaluation tool, and they will be aware of exactly how their essays will be graded.)

© Novel Units, Inc.   All rights reserved

Belle Prater's Boy
Answer Key
(Study Questions)

Chapters 1–2 (Pages 3–22)

1. Gypsy, the narrator, begins the novel by telling the story of Belle Prater's disappearance from Crooked Ridge in 1953. On page 16, the setting is Granny Ball's kitchen in Coal Station, Virginia, in April, 1954.
2. Gypsy Arbutus Leemaster
3. Belle Prater has disappeared.
4. Everett Prater, Woodrow's father, was drinking too much.
5. Gypsy is a beautiful girl who lives with her mother and stepfather in Coal Station, Virginia, next door to her grandparents. She lives in a nice 1950's house with all the conveniences. She is Woodrow's cousin. Gypsy's mother is Belle Prater's sister.
6. Gypsy does not like her stepfather.
7. Answers will vary.

Chapters 3–4 (Pages 23–38)

1. Granny and Grandpa Ball enjoy Woodrow and are very good to him. Answers will vary.
2. The men ask Woodrow about his mother and talk about Woodrow being cross-eyed. The men say it is a pity about what happened to Amos Leemaster. They also insult "the whole female gender." (page 30)
3. Gypsy's hair is a source of pride for Love, her mother. Gypsy wants short hair that would be easier to take care of.
4. Both can play the piano.
5. It is such a happy family party.
6. Answers will vary.
7. Answers will vary.

Chapters 5–6 (Pages 39–57)

1. Love, Belle's sister, took her boyfriend. Belle did not accept this easily. She acted impulsively and ran off to marry Everett Prater.
2. Belle wanted to get away from Coal Station and any reminder that Amos Leemaster had chosen her sister.
3. Answers will vary.
4.

Gypsy's Childlike Behavior	**Gypsy's Mature Behavior**
treatment of Porter	the way she talks to adults
nightmares, crying	
tucked into bed by her mother	

5. Mrs. Cooper insults Woodrow by saying he is "not much for looks"—just like his mama. Answers will vary. (page 52)
6. Woodrow wants straight eyes and his mama to come home. Gypsy wants short hair.

© Novel Units, Inc.   All rights reserved

Belle Prater's Boy
Answer Key
(Study Questions)

7. Woodrow is going to explain his mother's disappearance.
8. Answers will vary.

Chapters 7–8 (Pages 58–74)

1. Answers will vary.
2. Blind Benny walks the streets at night and goes through people's trash. Answers will vary.
3. Ed Morrell was a man in prison who was placed in a straitjacket. Belle Prater felt that she too was in a straitjacket being squeezed to death. She felt she had to get out.
4. Answers will vary.
5. Porter
6. Woodrow is helping Gypsy to "see things in a new light." (page 68)
7. Woodrow wins over the teacher and students with his stories and clever puzzles.
8. Answers will vary.

Chapters 9–10 (Pages 75–90)

1. Everett Prater comes to see how his son is doing. Woodrow is happy to see his dad, until after the visit he sees his dad get into the car with a "blond-headed woman." (pages 78–79)
2. The blond woman in his dad's car.
3. If Gypsy doesn't accept Porter's invitation, she will miss Grace Kelly and Jimmy Stewart. Grace Kelly is going to look in a window. This reminds Gypsy of something and she goes into hysterics.
4. Answers will vary.
5. Answers will vary.

Chapters 11–12 (Pages 91–109)

1. Answers will vary.
2. Amos named Gypsy Arbutus, or "Beauty."
3. Answers will vary.
4. Answers will vary.
5. Woodrow thinks his mother will contact him in the strange way of a strong force separating two dimensions.
6. Buzz and Woodrow tell stories. Buzz tries to hurt Woodrow by asking him if his mama was cross-eyed.
7. Answers will vary.

Belle Prater's Boy
Answer Key
(Study Questions)

Chapters 13–14 (Pages 110–123)

1. Woodrow is so much fun, tells so many stories, and treats everybody like they are special.
2. Amos had made Love promise never to cut Beauty's hair.
3. Answers will vary.
4. Woodrow gets very angry.
5. Examples: "twilight and dawn—places where dark and light meet" and "the moment between waking and sleeping" (page 122).
6. Answers will vary.
7. Answers will vary.

Chapters 15–16 (Pages 124–144)

1. The way Woodrow looks at things with fresh eyes makes Gypsy "see them fresh, too." (page 125)
2. Answers will vary.
3. Belle had insulted Mrs. Cooper in front of Mr. Cooper before they were married. She has never forgiven Belle.
4. Answers will vary.
5. Woodrow's daddy is so used to the taste, smell, and feeling of rum, he doesn't fall for that suggestion. Mrs. Cooper is not a drinker, so the "power of suggestion" works on her.
6. Woodrow seems to get away with things that Gypsy would be punished for.
7. Answers will vary.
8. "…don't ever have anything to do with a girl with long, golden hair. She'll tie you up in knots every time." (page 142) Gypsy feels that the story is pointed toward her.
9. Porter points out that both Belle and Gypsy are talented with music, are imaginative and creative.
10. She is trying to "find herself again." (page 144)
11. Answers will vary.

Chapters 17–18 (Pages 145–162)

1. The nightmares come more often but with less horror. Gypsy can almost recall what the nightmare is trying to tell her.
2. Buzz suggests that Woodrow tell the teacher about his mother's disappearance.
3. Answers will vary.
4. Gypsy says her father died in a fire, trying to save a baby.
5. Buzz says that Amos was so scarred in the fire that he shot himself in the face.
6. Gypsy leaves school on wobbly legs and goes home.
7. Gypsy is filled with rage at her father for killing himself. She wants to hurt him, so she cuts her hair—which her father had made Love promise never to cut.

© Novel Units, Inc.   All rights reserved

Belle Prater's Boy
Answer Key
(Study Questions)

8. Love sends Porter to find Gypsy. Porter treats Gypsy with understanding and respect.
9. Answers will vary.

Chapters 19–20 (Pages 163–174)
1. Gypsy and her mother had not talked about the suicide because they couldn't bear to. Gypsy couldn't stand to "look truth in the face."
2. Amos was in deep depression. He couldn't face his disfigurement.
3. Gypsy tries to get back at her father and feels her hair was like a veil that hid her real person.
4. Answers will vary.
5. Answers will vary.
6. She wants to show the world she is someone under the hair, and get back at Amos—but now she has to face her friends with her chopped-off hair.
7. Gypsy tells the girls she has the latest New York fashion.
8. Answers will vary.
9. Answers will vary.

Chapters 21–23 (Pages 175–196)
1. Benny becomes a "sin eater." (page 177) A superstition is a belief founded on irrational feelings, especially of fear, and marked by a trust in or reverence for charms, omens, signs, the supernatural, etc. Also, it includes any rite or practice inspired by such belief.
2. The Leemasters have provided a place for Benny to live and plenty to eat. He would no longer have to be a sin eater. People leave things for him on their doorsteps.
3. Gypsy remembers how Jesus might come to us in disguise. Blind Benny might be Jesus in disguise.
4. Gypsy would like to relive the night walk with Benny, while Woodrow would like to relive Porter's birthday party.
5. Gypsy kisses Benny.
6. Benny is able to see beyond appearances to what is really important.
7. Gypsy will have a formal piano recital. Woodrow's eyes will be examined in Baltimore.
8. Gypsy suffered the loss of her father and the terrible nightmares, even though she lives in a beautiful place.
9. Belle made up the story about a place in the air behind the house and other magical-place stories. Woodrow says he's known all the time that the stories weren't real.

© Novel Units, Inc.   All rights reserved

Belle Prater's Boy
Answer Key
(Study Questions) and (Student Activies)

10. Belle took some of Woodrow's clothes and $30 when she disappeared. Woodrow did not tell his father about the clothes and money because Woodrow did not think his father cared as much about Belle as he appeared to.
11. The farmer's conscience in the story of the golden hair, like Everett Prater's conscience, bothered him. Everett Prater's conscience bothered him because "he wasn't always good to her [Belle]." (page 195)
12. Woodrow hopes to find a message from his mother.
13. Both Belle and Amos left their children because "their pain was bigger than their love." (page 195)
14. The in-between feelings include:
    between being kids and grown-ups
    between summer and winter
    between dawn and a new day
    between sleeping and waking

Activity #1, Activity #2, and Activity #3:
These are open-ended activities with no specific answers. Time should be allotted for students to share and discuss their responses to these activities.

Activity #4:

Setting	Characters	Actions	Problems
	swashbuckling	stash	resolution
	immature	conjured	option
	reckless	dissected	
	invisible		

Nouns	Verbs	Adjectives	Adverbs
mattock	mesmerized	immature	
stash	conjured	reckless	
follicles	dissected	swashbuckling	
sedative	addled	invisible	
straitjacket		ample	
compulsion			
frenzy			
resolution			
option			
inevitable			

Belle Prater's Boy
Answer Key
(Student Activities)

Activity #5:
1. dedicated—means set apart for special use; the other words mean surprised.
2. burly—large body; the other words denote smallness.
3. disfigured—unsightly physical appearance; the other words describe character traits.
4. appendage—a part joined to; the other words are synonyms for the part of the body between the chest and the pelvis.
5. appeased—means to reduce or bring to peace; the other words are antonyms of appeased.
6. tranquilize—to calm; the other words are antonyms of *calm*.
7. premeditated—planned; the other words mean without plan or forethought.
8. stampede—sudden rushing or running movement; the other words mean slow, careful approach.
9. remember—to think about the past; the other words look to the future and new beginnings.
10. natural—the usual, not artificial; the other words describe the unusual.
11. avoidable—able to be evaded; the other words are antonyms, meaning cannot be prevented.
12. distasteful—offensive; the other words are antonyms, meaning pleasant, positive.
13. reward—something given or done in return; the other words are antonyms, meaning negative reactions.
14. sweet—agreeable to the taste or delightful to the mind; the other words are antonyms, meaning out of order and/or disordered condition.
15. repulsive—feeling of dislike or repugnance; the other words are antonyms with positive meanings of wonder and amazement.

© Novel Units, Inc.   All rights reserved

Belle Prater's Boy
Answer Key
(Student Activities)

Activity #6:

Word	Definition	Phonetic Spelling	Origin
agitate	to disturb or shake violently	(aj´ • ə • tāt)	L—*agitatus*
bombard	to attack with bombs, shells, or questions	(bom • bärd´)	OF—*bombarde* L—*bombus*
consumption	progressiove wasting of the body, esp. from tuberculosis	(kən • sump´• shən)	L—*consumptio*
disfigurement	marred or destroyed appearance	(dis • fig´• yər • mənt)	L—*dis + figurer* or *figurare*
elate	to excite	(i • lāt´)	L—*elatus*
exertion	strong action or effort	(ĕg • zûr´shən)	L—*exertus*
nonchalant	casually indifferent	(non´shə • lant) (non • shə • länt´)	L—*non + calere*
parasite	one who lives at another's expense	(par´ • ə • sīt)	L—*parasitus* G—*paraitos*
remorse	hopeless anguish caused by a sense of guilt	(ri • môrs´)	L—*remordere*
trek	slow journey	(trek)	Du—*trekken*

Activity #7:
1. Answers will vary.
2. Answers will vary.
3. in- (not, without)
   inter- (with each other, together, mutual, between)
   ex- (out of, lacking, former, forth)
   trans- (across, beyond, through, on the other side of)
   non- (not)
   dis- (away from, apart, the undoing of, deprivation of some quality, not)

Belle Prater's Boy
Answer Key
(Student Activities and Novel Tests)

Activities #8–14

These are open-ended activities with no specific answers. Time should be allotted for students to share and discuss their responses to these activities.

Novel Test—Vocabulary

1. E
2. O
3. H
4. J
5. B
6. L
7. M
8. F
9. Q
10. A
11. G
12. D
13. K
14. I
15. C

Novel Test—Objective

1. G
2. D
3. G
4. H
5. I
6. E
7. G
8. J
9. K
10. C
11. L
12. B
13. C
14. D
15. E

Novel Test—Identification by Quotation

1. Woodrow—p. 15
2. Love—p. 41
3. Gypsy—p. 55
4. Gypsy—p. 85
5. Benny—p. 87
6. Woodrow—p. 98
7. Buzz—p. 108
8. Benny—p. 94
9. Grandpa—p. 113
10. Woodrow—p. 137
11. Porter—p. 144
12. Woodrow—p. 150
13. Buzz—p. 155

Novel Test—Multiple Choice

1. C
2. D
3. D
4. A
5. B
6. B
7. D
8. C
9. A
10. C
11. B
12. C
13. B
14. C
15. B
16. D
17. C
18. A
19. B
20. B

© Novel Units, Inc.　　　All rights reserved

Belle Prater's Boy
Answer Key
(Novel Tests)

Novel Test—Short Answer/Essays

1. **Crooked Ridge**—home of the Praters
2. **tree house**—built by Amos for Beauty; used by Woodrow and Gypsy (Beauty)
3. **Granny Ball**—mother of Love and Belle; very deaf; has a way of talking to her grandchildren about important things; a kind and loving person
4. **Love**—beautiful woman; daughter of Grandpa and Granny Ball; took Belle's boyfriend, Amos Leemaster; remarried Porter Dotson; Gypsy's mother
5. **Porter**—married Love after Amos Leemaster's suicide; tries to be a good stepfather to Gypsy
6. **Mr. Collins**—the new seventh grade teacher at Coal Station School
7. **Mrs. Cooper**—had been insulted by Belle when she was in school; tries to hurt Woodrow's feelings; Woodrow tries an experiment of suggestion on her
8. **Gypsy**—narrator of the story; found her father after his suicide; can tell funny jokes; has beautiful hair; can play the piano; dislikes her stepfather
9. **Woodrow**—his mother, Belle Prater, has disappeared; very homely, cross-eyed boy who can tell funny stories and puzzles; wise about many things; has the key to Belle Prater's disappearance
10. **Belle Prater**—Woodrow's mother who has run away to escape her problems and to try to find herself; not a beautiful woman like her sister; married Everett Prater just to get married and leave home; talented musician and storyteller

Essays

Answers to essays will vary, and you will probably want to require more detail from higher-level students. Answers should be supported by references to and details from the novel.

A. The Main Conflicts in *Belle Prater's Boy*
- Belle: Inner conflict—She felt she was in a straitjacket. She left home trying to find herself. She was jealous of her sister, Love, and her many boyfriends, especially Amos Leemaster. She loved her son, Woodrow, but she wanted out of the life she had chosen. The reader does not learn if Belle has resolved her conflicts.
- Woodrow: Person vs. Person conflict with Buzz—not completely resolved. Conflict with society—doesn't tell the whole truth about his mother's disappearance at first. Person vs. Person conflict with Gypsy—resolved.
- Gypsy: Inner conflict—could not face the fact of her father's suicide—resolved. Person vs. Person conflict with Porter—resolved. Person vs. Person conflict with Woodrow—resolved.

Belle Prater's Boy
Answer Key
(Novel Tests)

B. *Porter and Gypsy*—Stepfathers have a hard time replacing or taking on the responsibilities of the missing parent. Porter tries. Gypsy gives Porter a hard time until she cuts her hair and she talks a bit to him. It will be resolved in time.
Grandpa and Granny Ball—They had tried hard to raise Belle and Love, but feel a certain amount of failure and sadness. They are good grandparents.
Love and Belle—Love promises if she ever sees Belle again she will make up for all the past hurts.
Woodrow and Gypsy—They become good friends for life.
Belle and Everett Prater—They did not work for or reach a happy marriage.

C. The author says that physical appearances are not all that important. The beauty inside, or the soul of the person, is what is important.

D. All the characters except Blind Benny change in the story. Answers will vary, but the changes must be supported by evidence from the book.

E. Comparison of Belle and Love—use the Venn diagram as preparation for writing the comparison.

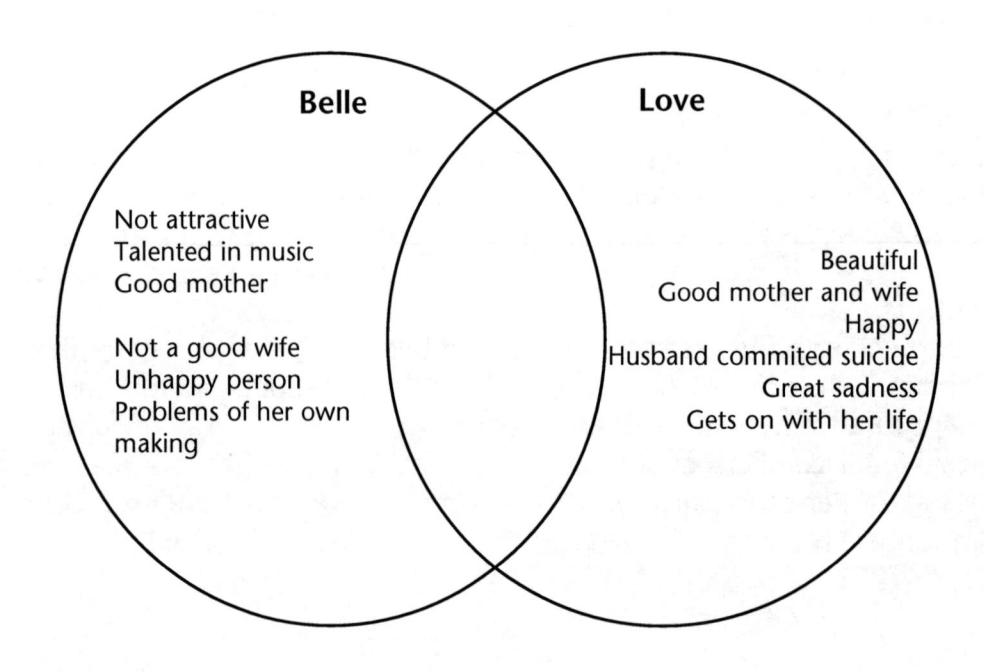

Belle
Not attractive
Talented in music
Good mother

Not a good wife
Unhappy person
Problems of her own making

Love
Beautiful
Good mother and wife
Happy
Husband commited suicide
Great sadness
Gets on with her life

© Novel Units, Inc.　　All rights reserved

Notes

Notes